Disciplining
Someone Else's Children
A Guide for Child Care Providers

Dr. Mattie L. Solomon

⊙iUniverse®

DISCIPLINING SOMEONE ELSE'S CHILDREN
A GUIDE FOR CHILD CARE PROVIDERS

iUniverse books may be ordered through booksellers or by contacting:

iUniverse
1663 Liberty Drive
Bloomington, IN 47403
www.iuniverse.com
1-800-Authors (1-800-288-4677)

Because of the dynamic nature of the Internet, any web addresses or links contained in this book may have changed since publication and may no longer be valid. The views expressed in this work are solely those of the author and do not necessarily reflect the views of the publisher, and the publisher hereby disclaims any responsibility for them.

Any people depicted in stock imagery provided by Thinkstock are models, and such images are being used for illustrative purposes only. Certain stock imagery © Thinkstock.

ISBN: 978-1-4917-6895-2 (sc)
ISBN: 978-1-4917-6894-5 (e)

Library of Congress Control Number: 2015908549

Print information available on the last page.

iUniverse rev. date: 06/03/2015

I dedicate this book to all the children
whose lives I have been blessed to touch.
I love you, and God loves you.

*Train up a child in the way he should go: and when he
is old, he will not depart from it.*

—Proverbs 22:6

Contents

Acknowledgments

I would like to thank all of the child-care providers and directors who trust me. Thank you for affording me the opportunity to glean an internal look at how children interact with their caregivers and peers. Thank you for your love of children and wanting to do your best on behalf of them.

Introduction

"If this were my child, I would ..." This is a familiar phrase commonly heard from someone confronting a discipline issue with someone else's child. What do you do when you feel a child left in your care is out of control? What do you do when you can't lean on what you felt worked with your own children, like a good spanking?

Child-care providers have to depend on their understanding of the social and emotional development of children to correct unwanted behavior. This book provides guidance for prevention and intervention in this area of child development. The following four areas that support effective discipline for preschool children are covered:

- understanding what discipline should be

- recognizing normal and abnormal behavior in preschoolers

- age-appropriate discipline strategies

- getting parents on the same page as child-care providers in the area of discipline

After spending many hours in several child-care facilities observing the interactions between teachers and the children in their care, I have found that teachers have a much easier time delivering an age-appropriate curriculum than they do implementing the strategies needed when dealing with a disruptive child.

The Merriam-Webster dictionary defines prevention as "the act or practice of stopping something bad from happening, the act of preventing or hindering." It defines intervention as "intervening to become involved in something (such as a conflict) in order to have an influence on what happens."

When a child disrupts the daily routine in a preschool, he or she is disrupting the learning process of other children. Although the focus of this book is on preschool-age children—preschool children are ages three to five years old—most child-care facilities care for infants, toddlers, and preschoolers.

Child-care providers have one of the most important jobs in the world. On a daily basis, they are responsible for our world's most valuable asset: our children. A child-care provider works in collaboration with parents as a child's first teacher.

Research has provided evidence that the first years of a child's life leave a lasting impression. The daily routines and activities of child-care facilities focus on the cognitive, social, and emotional development of children.

Discipline is a part of the social and emotional development of children and can hinder their progress if not dealt with appropriately. How do you prevent the learning of other children from being interrupted by disruptive behavior? And how do you intervene to stop disruptive behavior from getting out of control and becoming damaging to someone's child?

Discipline is crucial to the overall well-being of the child. How can child-care providers be sure they are doing the right things when it comes to this area of child development? Disciplining someone else's children is part of a child-care teacher's daily responsibility and a necessary part of creating a safe learning environment for all children.

Each child is unique and develops at his or her own rate, so there are mental, developmental, and exceptional needs issues that may require additional specialized guidance.

Chapter 1 of this book answers the question, what is discipline? By examining what discipline should be. Chapter 2 looks at research and other information to explore the behaviors of preschool children and determines essential ways to respond by recognizing normal and abnormal behavior. Chapter 3 promotes the importance of age-appropriate interaction with young children in the development of a socially and emotionally healthy child. When disciplining young children, child-care providers should utilize age-appropriate discipline strategies. Chapter 4 discusses the necessity of getting parents on the same page as child-care providers with regard to discipline.

Chapter 5 provides scenarios of discipline situations for reflection and discussion. These give the reader opportunities to examine alternative ways and strategies for correcting undesirable or disruptive behaviors. Chapter 5 also includes an interview with one child-care director on the topic of suspension.

The term *child-care facility* is used in this book when referring to facilities that care for young children before they become school-aged and attend kindergarten. Such facilities might be day care centers, preschools, child-care ministries, drop-in centers, and child-care learning centers.

The terms *child-care providers* or *child-care workers* refer to teachers, classroom assistants, teachers' assistants, or school directors.

Chapter 1

Understanding What Discipline Should Be

Chapter 1

Understanding What Discipline Should Be

Strategies for disciplining young children may be referred to in a number of ways, including *classroom management*, *setting limits*, *setting boundaries*, *redirection*, *teaching self-control*, and *teachable moments*. These terms and phrases are used in this book when referring to strategies to correct unwanted, disruptive, or undesirable behavior in young children.

This chapter will examine what discipline should be when implemented with young children.

The Merriam-Webster dictionary defines discipline as "control that is gained by requiring that rules or orders be obeyed—and punishing bad behavior." It's also defined as a way of behaving that shows a willingness to obey rules or orders.

The discipline policies used by child-care providers should be clear and should be shared with parents. Parents have many questions and concerns about discipline, and there should be a collaboration with the child-care providers that influences actions taken at home to correct behavior. Child-care providers have shared with me that their efforts to correct unwanted behavior fail when parents do not set the same expectations in the home. (Chapter 4 covers how to get parents on the same page as child-care providers with regard to discipline.)

One alarming concern is the practice of suspensions and expulsions of young children from child-care facilities. Suspension is an extreme disciplinary action because the child is removed from the learning environment for a short- or long-term period. Expulsions, in which the child is suspended permanently, are used in some cases. Does this type of discipline work? In chapter 5, I pose this question during an interview with the director of a child-care provider. Suspension of young children is the focus of my interview with her.

Disciplining young children requires clarification due to the damaging effects it can have if not administered correctly. I found that one way child-care providers clarify how they discipline is by providing a discipline policy. The providers' discipline policy is shared with child-care workers and parents.

The discipline policy makes very clear the responses to misbehavior that should not be done under any circumstance and the responses that are acceptable. Some examples of responses I saw on many of the child-care providers' discipline policies are described below.

These are responses that are *not* allowed:

- physical punishment

- threats or bribes

- basic needs withheld (such as food or water)

- humiliation

- isolation

- restraint

Acceptable responses to misbehavior include the following:

- redirecting the child to a new activity

- establishing clear classroom rules

- respecting the children

- being consistent in enforcing rules

- using positive language to explain behavior

- speaking calmly while bending down to the child at eye level

- moving child to timeout chair no more than one minute per year of the child's age, if necessary

Some teachers find it beneficial to predetermine how discipline issues should be handled.

Some of the predetermined methods used by teachers I visited include the following:

- time-out locations in the classroom

- a person outside the classroom (another teacher) to take them out when necessary

- sending them to the director

During my visits to some of the child-care facilities, I observed that many of the teachers had the tendency to use the same discipline actions over and over again whether they worked previously or not. They seemed to do this during times when they allowed themselves to become frustrated. I share these real-life observations in chapter 5, "Scenarios of Discipline Situations."

I have observed teachers using the following tactics:

- threatening to take away an activity they know the child enjoys (such as recess)

- yelling out the child's name over and over

- saying things that are meant to shame the child or make him or her feel guilty

- involving the other children in the classroom by using the child as an example of wrong or bad behavior

In the health article "It's Not Discipline. It's a Teachable Moment" by Tara Parker-Pope, the author quoted Dr. Kenneth Ginsburg, adolescent medicine specialist at children's hospital of Philadelphia who explain to parents the etymology of the word. The Latin root is "discipulus" which means student or pupil. He stated that when he tell parents this their faces say "It's not about punishment? It's about teaching?' That changes things."

I found that when discipline is used as punishment, teachers lose the opportunity to teach.

Some situations with children escalate into a child being disciplined (punished) that can be prevented. At each age and stage of development, children learn to manage their emotions and relationships. To learn how to do this, they must experience many life events and situations. Child-care providers are responsible for understanding and nurturing them through these situations.

Both spoiled children and children who are harshly disciplined are at risk for emotional and behavioral problems. Being consistent in the approach or discipline strategy can change the course of a child's development. How most children respond emotionally is determined by their age and stage of development. What might be perceived as misbehaving may just be a necessary teachable moment for a child.

The first step is to learn what is considered normal behavior for each age and stage of development. Recognizing normal and abnormal behavioral of children is the focus of chapter 2.

Chapter 2

Recognizing Normal and Abnormal Behavior in Preschoolers

Recognizing Normal and Abnormal Behavior in Preschoolers

How do I know if any of the preschool children in my care have abnormal behavior? The article "Normal Child Behavior" written by The American Academy of Pediatrics explained it as follows:

"The difference between normal and abnormal behavior is not always clear; usually it is a matter of degree or expectation. A fine line often divides normal from abnormal behavior, in part because what is 'normal' depends upon the child's level of development, which can vary greatly among children of the same age. Development can be uneven too, with a child's social development lagging behind his intellectual growth, or vice versa. In addition, 'normal' behavior is in part determined by the context in which it occurs—that is, by the particular situation and time, as well as by the child's own particular family values and expectations, and cultural and social background."

Understanding a child's individual developmental progress is important in order to understand, accept, or correct his or her behavior (as well as the response of the teacher). Remember—children have differences in temperament, development, and behavior.

An important part of discipline is knowing whether to intervene or let children be children. Safety is the first priority, and danger needs immediate action. It is the responsibility of the child-care providers to teach children, directly or indirectly. This may mean stopping or redirecting a child's undesirable behavior for his or her safety or the safety of other children.

During my visits to several child-care providers' facilities, I observed that many teachers faced challenging behaviors during playtime. I noticed that teachers' frustrations could often have been avoided by understanding what children were experiencing developmentally during play. A Child Action, Inc. article titled "The Importance of Play" discusses how children's behavior in play develops in stages: "Play allows children to explore new things at their own pace, master physical ability, learn new skills and figure things out in their own way." During play with others, children learn leadership skills by directing the action or by following a leader. The following are common stages of play:

- onlooker behavior: watching what other children are doing but not joining in the play

- solitary play: playing alone without regard for others; being involved in independent activities like art or playing with blocks or other materials

- parallel activity: playing near others but not interacting, even when using the same play materials

- associative play: playing in small groups with no definite rules or assigned roles

- cooperative play: deciding to work together to complete a building project or pretend play with assigned roles for all of the members of the group

Learning to share is a process that takes several years to develop, and children will need proper supervision by adults to master this skill. If children do not master this skill, their reactions could be the cause of discipline concerns. The following are three stages of development for learning to share:

- first stage: children think everything is *theirs*.

- second stage: children discover that some things belong to others.

- third stage: children know they can lend a toy and get it back. Children are more likely to share when they see their toys come back to them and when other children share *their* toys.

During play, children also increase their social competence and emotional maturity. Smilansky and Shefatya (1990) contend that school success largely depends on children's ability to interact positively with their peers and adults. Play is vital to children's social development.

Play supports emotional development by providing a way to express and cope with feelings (Isenberg and Jalongo, 2014). The importance of play in children's lives is well documented. As children grow and change, play develops with them according to a developmental sequence.

As we see, playtime is a necessary learning activity for children. Teachers would be wise to use this time to teach children many valuable social skills.

Some preschoolers may have tantrums. Their tantrums should not be as severe as a two-year-old's tantrums, because they should be gaining more control over their emotions. They also may display aggressive behavior, but should be learning to use their words instead of acting on their impulses.

Teachers should be concerned when children exhibit behaviors that professionals consider to be outside of normal misbehavior.

It is normal for preschoolers to try to gain more independence. For example, they may argue and exercise their right to say no. Preschoolers also want to have the freedom that big kids have while still craving the degree of attention that babies get. The following warning signs of abnormal behavior are described in an article by child pediatricians (American Academy of Pediatrics):

❖ difficulty managing emotional outbursts

❖ difficulty managing impulses (such as physical aggression and verbal impulses)

❖ behavior that does not respond to discipline (It is normal for children to continue to repeat misbehavior from time to time. They do this to see if the care provider will follow through with discipline.)

❖ misbehavior that does not respond to appropriate disciplinary action

❖ behavior that interferes with school and causes a child to fall behind academically

❖ behavior that interferes with social interactions with others

❖ behavior that causes self-injury or talk of suicide

Some behaviors listed previously may be a sign of abnormal behavior. However, more serious than these behaviors are ones that are harmful or may cause death.

A mental health professional needs to evaluate children who slam their hands or fists into walls, bang their heads, cut or burn themselves, or talk about wanting to die or kill themselves.

It is critical that child-care workers such as teachers know the principle of children's age-appropriate behaviors so that appropriate responses are given to redirect undesirable behavior—and so that children can be referred to professionals for evaluation or support when needed. Teachers should inform the child-care facility directors of any concerns they may have concerning a child's behavior. The director will then share these concerns with parents.

One definition of *age appropriate* generally refers to activities that fall into the range of appropriateness for a given age group. Things that are considered appropriate are toys, curriculum, behavior, and skills. Child-care providers often refer to activities as age-appropriate. For example, threading beads is an appropriate activity for preschoolers but not for infants.

Are there age-appropriate ways to respond to the behavior issues of children? Chapter 3 provides insight into different strategies to address the issue of age-appropriate discipline.

Chapter 3

Age-Appropriate Discipline Strategies

Chapter 3

Age-Appropriate Discipline Strategies

During my observations at the child-care facilities, I found discipline to be a challenge for many of the teachers. Correcting undesirable behavior is a necessary part of the social development of children. The way children are communicated with and responded to has to be age-appropriate. I mention this term repeatedly because of the importance it plays in understanding and teaching young children.

As a member of The National Association for the Education of Young Children (NAEYC), I am a firm believer in their philosophy that for child-care providers to be effective, their strategies in all areas of early learning should be age-appropriate. Information I obtained from NAEYC's online resource describes *developmentally-appropriate practice* (DAP) as appropriate teaching. This is based on research on how children develop and learn in effective early education. The NAEYC DAP approach involves teachers meeting children at their age and stage of development. Accomplishing this can help each child meet challenges and achieve learning to his or her potential.

I also observed that preschool children learn best when their teachers develop positive and caring relationships with them. Much research shows that children learn best in safe, trusting, learning environments and that children will respond positively when they receive age-appropriate, carefully planned guidance and assistance.

Developing a trusting relationship with preschool children is essential to their emotional and social growth. I have also discerned that it is just as important for a child-care worker (director, teacher,

teacher assist, and so forth) to gain the trust of the children in their care as it for the children to have gained trust for their parents. Child-care workers have a responsibility to initiate and develop this trusting relationship.

A trusting relationship can be developed and maintained by providing children with opportunities, letting them know they are cared for and safe, and treating them with respect. The way to provide opportunities is by allowing them to do things that they want to do and not limiting them. Let children try new things and new ways of doing things. It is the teacher's responsibility to keep them safe by monitoring and facilitating the activity. Allowing children to explore is a way to build trust.

I have observed that teachers who create a safe learning environment in the classroom are most often more relaxed. They are comfortable with allowing children to make their own choices from classroom activities (such as dramatic play) or work stations (such as one with manipulatives). This allows children to have a sense that the teacher trusts them and is willing to let them learn on their own.

As the teacher monitors the children, he or she has confidence that even if a child gets in trouble, the situation can be a healthy learning experience for them—or maybe even a teachable moment. Children need and want to know that they are important. Children learn to trust when teachers let them know that they care about them no matter what … even if they get in trouble.

When redirecting or stopping undesirable behavior, the teacher can demonstrate that they care about the child by giving him or her a task to do, such as letting them be a helper for the day. This sends the message: *I do not care for your behavior, but I do care about you.*

"Let yes mean yes and no mean no." I know you may have heard this saying before, but it is very important when communicating with young children. Being consistent with responses is the key. I find that preschool children will respond to expectations because they want to please. The rules should not change on a day-to-day basis depending on the teacher's mood.

Children should know what to expect even if they get in trouble. When undesirable behavior has a consequence, the consequence should be communicated clearly and carried out. Yes, even carrying out a consequence builds trust, meaning *consequences to correct undesirable behavior* not *threats*.

In the same way, promises should be kept. If, for example, the teacher makes a promise to give extra recess time or a treat to children who complete a task, the teacher should follow through with the promise. Breaking a promise can have a damaging effect on building a trusting relationship. I believe and have seen that when preschool children have a trusting relationship with their teachers, they bounce back more easily and quickly from adverse and challenging situations.

Children should learn the following skills from age-appropriate discipline:

- how to recognize and express feelings

- how to problem solve

- anger management

- self-discipline

- impulse control

- social skills

The following actions or comments are not constructive toward building a trusting relationship with children.

- frustration and/or anger

- belittling comments

- physical grabbing

- threatening comments and/or gestures

Young children need the help of loving parents and child-care providers to develop strong, secure, trusting, and bonded relationships from infancy through age three. If they develop correctly, the independence they want as toddlers will be balanced. However, when they reach school age, they will continue to need the support of parents and teachers to build more and more confidence and trust in themselves.

I have observed many teachers who take advantage of using daily situations as opportunities to teach children. I, like other professional educators, call these times *teachable moments*. Because of the stage of development of preschoolers, teachable moments can be very effective.

Through my reading and research, I discovered that the concept of teachable moment was popularized by Robert Havighurst in his 1952 book, *Human Development and Education*, in which he referred to a *teachable moment* as the ability to learn a particular task when the timing is right. He stated: "It is important to keep in mind that unless the time is right, learning will not occur."

I define *disciplinary teaching moments* as when unexpected unacceptable or undesirable behavior happens with a child or group of children that can be used by the teacher as an opportunity to teach or even model proper responses.

> For example: Two children playing together begin to fight over a toy. The teacher uses this moment to teach the children how to share.

As mentioned earlier, it is essential that parents and child-care providers share in helping children develop strong, secure, trusting, and bonded relationships. It is imperative for children's social emotional development that parents support the efforts of their child-care providers to correct undesirable and disruptive behavior. They have to be on the same page to get appropriate results. The next chapter will examine ways that providers can involve parents in this endeavor.

Chapter 4

Getting Parents on the Same Page with Discipline

Getting Parents on the Same Page with Discipline

Many of the child-care providers I spoke with shared the frustration of not having support from the children's parents, especially with discipline issues. They shared that the parents seemed to be at a loss as to how to correct undesirable disruptive behavior when it happened at home, and they looked to them for advice and answers.

Much research has been done and many articles and books have been written on the topic of *parental involvement*. I wrote a book titled "Missing Link?" in which I interviewed many parents. I asked them: "Do you feel that you are missing in the educational process of your children? If so, then why?" The book shared their perspectives on this important issue.

From the discussions with parents in "Missing Link?" I found that parents need to be empowered, and to be empowered they need to be informed. They need to be included to play an active, effective role in what happens at their children's school. This will mean that the schools should provide the resources and support that parents need—such as time management and parenting classes—to ensure that parents are equipped with the necessary tools.

Parents need to be available to play an active role in their children's education to ensure that they receive what they need to be successful academically and socially. Communication with parents is critical.

Some of the behavior I observed in children with discipline issues seemed to stem from anger. They would often respond to other children or their teacher with anger. I therefore thought it would be beneficial for preschools to provide workshops for parents on conflict management and anger management. Parents are role models for their children. Children respond to situations in the same way they see their parents respond.

Child-care providers have long known how important the role of parents is in the social, emotional, and cognitive development and well-being of children. I believe that they have to be on the same page at some point to produce successful children who become productive, well-balanced adults.

Discipline strategies used in the child-care facilities need to be consistent with strategies used by parents. As I mentioned earlier, discipline needs to be consistent. Consistency cannot happen if the preschool defines undesirable or unacceptable behavior as one thing and children demonstrate this behavior at home without receiving the same redirections or consequences they get at preschool. What can child-care providers do? Some ideas follow:

- The first step may be to have parents take part in the development of the discipline policy and procedures. If one already exists, invite parents to a review and revision of the existing discipline policy.

- Ask parents to incorporate the discipline strategies used at the child-care facility at home, such as consequences, redirection, teachable moments, love, and so forth.

- Create and/or provide a journal for parents to note how they respond to disciplinary situations at home.

- Instead of suspending (expelling a child permanently), give parents the opportunity to attend parenting sessions on discipline.

In chapter 5, the issue of suspension is discussed in an interview with a child-care facility director. The director gave her perspective on suspending young children.

Chapter 5 also provides scenarios of discipline situations that can be used for personal reflection or to stimulate discussions.

Chapter 5

Scenarios of Discipline Situations

Chapter 5

Scenarios of Discipline Situations

Several child-care facility directors expressed concerns pertaining to the many discipline issues they have with the children in their preschools. They conveyed even more apprehension over the way their child-care workers sometimes respond to the children during disciplinary situations.

They asked me for suggestions and strategies to aid with this growing concern. Because of my desire to support them, I was motivated to view firsthand what was happening. I asked them for permission to come to the facilities to observe the interactions between the children and their teachers and other child-care workers. I also wanted to observe the way the children interacted with each other.

I was granted permission to observe by several facilities. The child-care workers were told that I was coming to observe but were not told the specifics of what I was observing. As I observed, I made journal entries of my observations.

I used journal entries to remember events later to help me determine the type of needs a facility had and the type of support I could provide. This book is a reflection of my desire to provide child-care workers and others with knowledge and a better understanding of how to respond to the actions of young children. The following scenarios are not intended to portray any of the children or child-care workers at the sites I observed but to give insight into what can happen when appropriate or inappropriate methods for discipline are used.

I would also like to direct the reader's attention to the information shared in the previous parts of this book. This information can then be used to reflect on the answers to the questions at the end of each scenario. The identities of the children, parents, child-care facilities, and workers are fictional. It is my intention to portray some circumstances that may happen in any preschool across the country.

Scenario #1

A Child-Care Facility in Omaha

The teacher started what appeared to be the daily morning routine. The children led the Pledge of Allegiance as parents continued to drop off their children. As this morning routine continued, one of the young boys did not want to cooperate.

The teacher said to him, "I guess you don't want a treat today." The little boy continued not to follow the pledge and lay over his chair and on to the floor. The teacher grabbed his hand and said, "Behave." He did not stop; he continued to sit in his chair and not participate.

The little boy continued to get attention from the other children by talking, playing on the floor, and running around the room. The teacher tried to stop him, and with every correction she touched, pulled, or grabbed him. Thirty minutes passed, and the teacher still had her attention on the little boy, holding him by the hand as she struggled to continue the daily routine. The teacher lifted him up by his elbows and placed him in the chair.

The teacher continued to go after the little boy, placing him in the chair and loudly saying, "I'm not playing with you." The teacher then said, "No treat for you today." This got the child's attention for a few seconds; he stopped to think about it and then yelled out and ran again. The teacher said, "No recess for you."

Some of the other children tried to get the little boy to stop acting out. The teacher began to chastise the other children who tried to stop him.

The teacher said in a frustrated voice, "Little boy, you are being a clown today." The teacher made several more attempts to sit him in the chair. She said, "I need to call some parents," which she never did. Then the little boy decided to hit a little girl, and she told the teacher. The teacher told the little girl to ignore him and that she would be okay.

The other children now had frowns on the faces, and one by one they tried to stop the little boy from acting out. Each one who tried—including a little boy who was hit in the head by him—were all told to ignore him.

About thirty-five minutes passed. The little boy continued to hit at the other children and made another little girl cry. The teacher said, "You have pushed me to my limits."

Forty-five minutes had passed. The teacher pushed the little boy into the chair and said, "You are pushing my buttons." The other children were now getting in trouble with the teacher because they were laughing at what he was doing.

1. What could the teacher have done without touching the little boy in the ways that she did? (grabbing and pushing)

2. What could the teacher have done at the start with his behavior?

3. Did the little boy disrupt the learning of the other children?

4. What could the teacher do to take back control of the classroom?

Scenario #2

A Child-Care Facility in Boston

All of the children were following the teacher's directions and paying attention to her. The teacher spoke in a loud voice whenever she addressed the children.

The teacher told the children, "It is now playtime." During this free time, the children danced and jumped around the room. The teacher changed the activity after ten to fifteen minutes. A little girl hit her elbow on a table. She then pointed to the table, went over to the teacher, and accused a little boy of hitting her.

The teacher grabbed the little boy who was accused by the arm and said, "Don't do that." Then she placed him in the corner and leaned over very close to him, her nose almost touching his. "You need to apologize," she told him, grabbing his arm. She kept him in the corner because he did not want to apologize. Speaking in a loud voice the teacher said, "I will have to talk to your parents tonight!" The little boy sat down in the corner with his head on the floor. The teacher picked him up from the floor and made him stand beside her.

The teacher held him by the wrist as she continued the next activity with the children. The teacher was still holding the little boy by the wrist throughout the activity, making him stand next to her. At times he tried to sit down, but the teacher pulled him up under his arms as she continued the activity with the other children.

The other children watched what was going on as they recited numbers. The teacher said, "Are you goofing off—being silly?" After about fifteen minutes, the teacher let go of the little boy and yelled at him, "Put on your shoes!" Another little boy asked the teacher, "Are you going to call the police too?" The teacher seemed frustrated.

For the next activity the children sat at their seats. The teacher continued to direct them using a loud tone of voice. Children were being cooperative and obediently followed the teacher's directions. The teacher was frustrated and yelled at students who asked her questions.

1. Did the children cause the teacher to lose control of the classroom?

2. What was going on with the little boy and the teacher?

3. What could the teacher have done differently with the little boy?

Scenario #3

A Child-Care Facility in Texas

The teacher turned off the television, looked at the children, and said, "You know what that means!" At that prompt, all the children stood up and started singing a song, and then they sang a marching song. As they sang, the teacher went to the kitchen—which was only a few feet away—to prepare a snack for them.

All the children knew the words and were very proud to sing. Singing was a part of their morning routine. As the children continued the routine, one little girl started to pull on the zipper of her jacket. The teacher said, "What did I tell you about that? Do you mess with your zipper during morning activities?" The little girl stopped and continued the routine with the rest of the children.

Another little girl started to pull at her finger. The teacher stopped the routine and said, "Stop pulling on your finger." She stopped, but then when she pulled on her finger again the teacher said, "What did I tell you? Leave it alone. Do you want to lose some of your recess?" Then the children started another routine in which they took turns reading out loud. During this activity, three other children were scolded or corrected by the teacher for things like rubbing the chair, pulling at a sleeve, and sliding down in the chair.

One little girl was corrected for the way she was sitting in her chair. The teacher then made all of the children practice how to sit in a chair correctly. One little boy slid down in his chair, and the teacher said in a loud voice, "Little boy, you are going to try me today? Don't go there. Do you want to lose your recess? Don't go there. Not today."

A little girl was dropped off late into the classroom. As soon as she came in she took a seat. The teacher stopped the activity she had started with the other children and asked her, "Were you throwing rocks at the other children during recess yesterday?" The little girl said "No, ma'am."

The teacher asked each child in the room one at a time, "Did you see her throwing rocks yesterday?" Each child responded, "Yes, ma'am." The teacher then turned to the little girl and said, "You are telling me that all of these children are lying on you? Stand up." She stood up, and the teacher asked her again, "Were you throwing rocks?" She said, "No, ma'am." The teacher responded, "How are all these children saying that you did that?" The teacher asked all of the children, "What is the rule?" She told the little girl, "Sit down no recess for you today."

The children continued to complete over five different activities to get the day started, and this took about forty-five to fifty minutes. The teacher became extremely uncomfortable and complained when any of the children did any small movement or gesture other than the motions that were a part of the activity.

1. Describe the environment created by the teacher in this classroom.

2. What message was the teacher giving to the little girl who was accused of throwing rocks?

3. How do you think the little girl felt when the teacher was talking to her and the other children concerning the rock-throwing incident?

4. How do you think the other children felt about the teacher involving them in the rock-throwing incident?

Scenario #4

A Child-Care Facility in Indiana

Two adults—one teacher and one teacher's assistant—were interacting with the children in a classroom. The children were involved in different activities; some were drawing with the teacher at a long table, while others were at a play area with the assistant.

One little girl started to kick a small dollhouse in the play area. The assistant said, "We don't kick things," but the little girl continued to kick it. After repeating "we don't kick things" three more times, the assistant picked her up because she continued to kick. After about five minutes, she put the little girl down, but she started to kick at the dollhouse again.

The teacher came in the play area while the girl was still kicking. She looked at the little girl and started to count, "One, two, three." By the time she got to three, the girl had stopped kicking. The teacher said, "Good job," and then she gave her a toy to play with. The teacher went back to the table with the other children who were drawing.

A little boy who had gotten off track was pulling at another little boy at the table. The teacher called him by name, and when he looked toward her she touched her nose. The little boy stopped what he was doing and touched his nose to show the teacher that she had his attention. The teacher redirected him (without touching him), and her voice level never escalated. She said (without yelling), "Bring your paper and come sit by me." He followed her directions, and she said, "Good job!"

1. Why did the little girl respond to the teacher and not the assistant?

2. Was this the first time the teacher responded to the children the way she did?

3. If not, then what led you to conclude that it was not the first time?

4. If yes, then what led you to conclude that it was the first time?

Interview with a child-care facility director

One concern that many child-care providers have is the use of suspension in response to the behavior of young children. I have spoken to several child-care directors who have reluctantly suspended children with the intent of changing undesirable, disruptive behavior. Suspension is when children are sent home with their parents or guardian, and they are not allowed to attend school for a period of time. Suspension is usually the result of the child's behavior.

I wanted to understand the effectiveness of suspending children from child-care facilities with young children. For this reason, I asked for and was granted an interview with one of the directors of a preschool. The director agreed to answer questions I had developed to explore this issue. The following are my questions and the responses from the director, whom I will refer to as *Director Ms. Care* (or just *director*), as I am keeping her true identity confidential.

Interview with a child-care facility director:

Me:

Director Care, what age group of children have you had to suspend from your child care?

Director (Ms. Care):

The youngest child was age two. Children are suspended mostly because of continual fighting with the other children or when we cannot get the parents to help with the situation. Some children bit when they fought with the other children. One of the discipline rules of our facility is *three bites and you are suspended*.

We actually gave one child more than three chances to change her behavior. This child bit up to ten times. We suspended the child for two days.

Me:

How did the parents react to the child being suspended?

Director:

They were a little upset but not surprised, because we gave them plenty of warnings concerning the child biting and fighting.

Me:

Did the suspension change the child's behavior?

Director:

No, not really. When the child came back, the biting and fighting continued. We realize that biting is an issue with some two-year-olds, but children who are three and still biting become a concern.

Me:

Does suspension work in your opinion?

Director:

Suspension sometimes works ... for example, one child hit a teacher and was throwing toys. The child was suspended for a day, came back, and was calm for about a week but then went through the same behavior and process of suspension again.

Me:

As the director, what role do you play in the decision to suspend a child?

Director:

In most cases the teacher will call for me to come to get the child who is acting out of control in a classroom. I will go get the child out of the room and take him or her to my office. Parents are then called and told to come get the child immediately. About 80 percent of the parents will or can come immediately. Some of the children have to sit in my office to wait for them.

When children are out of control to the point that no redirection or discipline will correct or stop the behavior, parents are usually asked to take them home for the day.

It is the extreme situations that caused the child to be suspended for longer periods of time, such as biting or throwing things at the teacher or other children.

Me:

What is the cause of children getting out of control?

Director:

I have found that most children want to please their teacher. They act out when they have not bonded with the teacher or when they don't feel like the teacher cares about them.

When I go to the classroom to get a child the teacher has called me to remove, the first thing I try to do is give the child a hug. I hug them and love on them and comfort them. The child will respond in a positive way because they trust me, and I can often get them to go back in the classroom without any other incident that day.

The child has gotten some loving from me, and that settles them down. I try to be an example ... some teachers get it, and some don't.

I have not seen evidence that the suspensions really work. It seems to be just to relieve the teacher of the aggressiveness of a child who is out of control for whatever reason.

We will suspend a child permanently if they are a danger to themselves or others. I love them all, and I do not like to suspend our children.

My reflection after the interview with the child-care director:

It is my experience that most child-care directors use suspension as a last alternative to correct behavior. This action is usually taken to get the attention of parents and to make them aware of the seriousness of the problems they are having with a child. This action may also be used as an example to the other children that certain behavior will not be tolerated.

Whenever I ask a child-care facility owner or director to share their perspective on the suspension of young children, I first notice a facial expression that reveals a sense of dismay as they proceed to share the instances that led them to suspend a child. I found that they are very much aware of the fact that children need to be in a safe learning environment and that suspending them may be taking them away from what they need.

They tell me that the needs of all the children in their care have to be taken into consideration. It is for this reason that they do what is necessary and hope that parents understand and that the children learn that they love them but that certain behavior is not conductive to learning and will not be tolerated.

- After reading the interview with the child-care director, take time to reflect and share your perspective on the suspension of young children from preschool.

- Reflect on the incidences that you are aware of concerning this issue.

Conclusion

Chapter 1 of this book examined what discipline should be by embracing what it should *not* be. No two children are alike, which makes it imperative that child-care workers take time to get to know the temperament and character of each of the children left in their care. Discipline should be used as an opportunity to *teach*, not to punish or belittle. Teachers should consider their motives when correcting undesirable behavior. There are some questions to stop and reflect on: What can I do to help children learn from what has happened? What type of example will my actions be for children?

Chapter 2 gave examples of normal and abnormal behavior in preschoolers. The challenges that child-care workers face to recognize the occurrence of abnormal preschooler behavior are examined, and actions to be taken when they suspect that something is wrong or abnormal are provided.

Playtime is an emotional time for young children, which makes it an ideal time to teach some important social and emotional skills.

Age-appropriate activity is not only academic but should be practiced when deciding what discipline strategy to use. Chapter 3 examined the rationale behind why all child-care activity should be developmentally appropriate. Consistency is a word echoed throughout this book. Chapter 4 challenges child-care providers to get parents on the same page with discipline. To ensure that discipline is effective, there has to be consistency between actions taken at home and at school to correct undesirable and disruptive behavior.

Scenarios are often used in many publications to provide a way to reflect on situations. In chapter 5 they are not only used to reflect but also to provide an opportunity to examine the consequences of what can happen when inappropriate interactions happen with young children. Discipline strategies discussed in this book can be utilized to determine a different outcome to the scenarios.

It is my desire that this book will touch the lives of many children in a positive way. I hope it serves as a guide to child-care workers because they have been given the important mission of developing socially and emotionally healthy children.

Mattie Lee Solomon, PhD, for over 20 years, Dr. Solomon has been involved in the education of countless Indianapolis children and adults, including over 20 years of work as a teacher and a school administrator (e.g. principal). Currently the Chair of the Humanities Department at Martin University in Indianapolis, Indiana Dr. Solomon serves as the Director of the Early Childhood Education Department which afforded her the opportunity to oversee the development of a child care service for the children of the university's students. Her abundance of experience training and supporting child care providers motivated her to pen, "Disciplining Someone Else's Children" A guide for Child Care Providers, which is a guide to discipline preschool children.

The richness of her experience with children and parents inspired her to pen her first book "Missing Link?" It documents various parents' perspectives concerning the education of their children?

Dr. Solomon's second book "What Did Your Parent Do to You" reveals true stories that opens windows to how childhood experiences influence the journeys people take thru life as well as how they parent.

Dr. Solomon earned a K-12 Business Education Teacher degree from the University of Indianapolis; a Master's degree in K-12 Educational Administration from Ball State University, Muncie, Indiana; and a PhD in the Philosophy of Education from Indiana State University, Terra Haute, Indiana.

Resources

1. J.P. Isenberg, M. R. Jalongo, *Creative Thinking and Arts-Based Learning Preschool through Fourth Grade,* (Merrill, an imprint of Pearson Education Inc., 2006), 53-55.

2. J.P. Isenberg and M. R. Jalongo, "Why is Play Important?" *Social and Emotional Development, Physical Development, Creative Development,* (April 2014).

3. Child Action Inc., *The Importance of Play,* 916/369-D191, www.childaction.org

4. Kendra Chery, *Child Behavioral Warning Signs to Watch For,* http://www.psychology.about.com/od/childcare/p/warning-signs.htm

5. NAEYC (National Association for the Education of Young Children) Developmentally Appropriate Practice (DAP) 2009, http:// www.naeyc.org/DAP

6. Dan Gartrell, *The Power of Guidance,* Teaching Social-Emotional Skills in Early Childhood Classrooms (2003).

7. Tara Parker-Pope, *It's Not Discipline, It's a Teachable Moment*, September 14, 2008 http://www.nytimes.com/2008/09/15/health/healthspecial12/15discipline

8. American Academy of Pediatrics, *A Parent's Guide to Building Resilience in Children and Teens: Giving Your Child Roots and Wrings*, Oct 2006

9. Jane Nelen, Ed.D & Cheryl L. Erwin M.A., *Positive Discipline-For Child Care Providers, A Practical & Effective Plan for Preschool & Day Care* (2002 1st edition Prima Publishing Company).

10. Mattie Lee Solomon PhD, *Missing Link?* (iUniverse, 2008).

Printed in the United States
by Baker & Taylor Publisher Services